ISBN 4-590-00086-5

Published by The Hokuseido Press
3-32-4, Honkomagome, Bunkyo-ku, Tokyo

ONE HUNDRED POEMS
FROM
ONE HUNDRED POETS

*Being a Translation of the Ogura
Hyaku-nin-isshiu*

BY
H. H. HONDA

THE   HOKUSEIDO   PRESS

WORDS OF COMMENDATION

One hundred little poems of Old Japan collected in an anthology during the Kamakura era are still alive in the memory of our literate people. These are pathetic effusions of the human heart which transcends racial differences, and, since the abolition of our isolation policy, they have been waiting about a century for their début in the international society in a proper costume.

Indeed, some attempts to give them the opportunity have already been made, of which the fruit of Mr. Honda's previous experiment was a significant instance. Now this same translator, himself a poet, has at last succeeded in giving these classical poems a most attractive new dress in the lovely attire of neat quatrains embellished with full rhyme.

I think I shall not be deceived in my expectation that these lyrics, which have stood the test of time, will prove, in this exotic make-up, to be the source of enjoyment for years to come to many lovers of poems of the heart both at home and abroad.

MINORU TOYODA

December 5, 1956

FOREWORD

The *Ogura Hyaku-nin-isshiu* or "One Hundred Poems From One Hundred Poets" were selected in the third decade of the thirteenth century. As to the person responsible for compiling this anthology there are two different opinions. Many give credit to Fujiwara-no-Sadaiye, whose song appears on Page 97, while others maintain Priest Rensho, a contemporary of the said Sadaiye, is the real compiler.

These verses are ranged in approximately chronological order: the first poem was written by the Emperor Tenchi who ruled from 668–671, and the last by the retired Emperor Juntoku whose last year of reign was 1221, so that more than five centuries come between them.

Almost all Japanese know these poems by heart, so that when they hear the upper part, i.e. the first two lines of the song, read, they are reminded of the lower part, i.e. the last two lines. Thus we have a time-honoured game played with these hundred verses on cards.

It is hoped the reader will find pleasure in the present translation.

My thanks are due to Dr. Minoru Toyoda for his kind recommendation, and to Mr. William E. Gilkey, the musician, who, besides giving me good advice, kindly read through the manuscript.

H. H.

November 15, 1956

わかころも
てはつゆに
ぬれ

かも
よか
なか
をひ

ふし

ふ
ね
に

ふり

天智天皇
秋の田の
かりほの庵の
苫をあらみ
我が衣手は
露にぬれつつ

柿本人麻呂
あしびきの
山鳥の尾の
しだり尾の
ながながし夜を
ひとりかもねむ

山部赤人
田子の浦に
打ち出でて
みれば
白妙の
富士の高嶺に
雪はふりつつ

をとめのす
かたしはし

とど

てか
いつ

はな

ほひ
しの

僧正遍昭
天つ風
雲のかよひ路
ふきとぢよ
乙女のすがた
しばしとどめむ

中納言兼輔
みかの原
わきて流るる
いづみ川
いつ見きとてか
戀しかるらむ

紀貫之
人はいさ
心もしらず
ふるさとは
花ぞむかしの
香ににほひける

みた

かこちか
なるわかな

やく
ほの

かほ
れ

なり

あるむかし

な
ほ

西行法師
なげけとて
月やは物を
おもはする
かこちがほなる
わがなみだかな

權中納言定家
こぬ人を
まつほの浦の
夕なぎに
やくやもしほの
身もこがれつつ

順德院
百敷や
古き軒端の
しのぶにも
なほあまりある
むかしなりけり

ころもほす
てふあまの
かく

せ
わか
ふ
る
いか
しか
け

持統天皇
春すぎて
夏きにけらし
白妙の
衣ほすてふ
天の
香具山

小野小町
花のいろは
うつりにけりな
いたづらに
わが身世にふる
ながめせしまに

右大將道綱母
歎きつつ
ひとりぬる夜の
明くる間は
いかに久しき
ものとかは知る

いまひとた
ひのあふこ
とも
く
にし
つき
みよ
まち
はし

和泉式部
あらざらむ
この世のほかの
おもひ出に
今一度の
逢ふこともがな

紫式部
めぐりあひて
見しやそれとも
わかぬ間に
雲隠れにし
夜半の月かな

小式部内侍
大江山
生野の道の
とほければ
まだふみも見ず
天の橋立

けふここの
へににほひ
ぬる
ゆる
よに
か
しの
もと

伊勢大輔
いにしへの
奈良の都の
八重櫻
けふ九重に
匂ひぬるかな

清少納言
夜をこめて
鳥の空音は
はかるとも
よにあふさかの
關はゆるさじ

式子内親王
玉の緒よ
絶えなば絶えね
ながらへば
しのぶることの
よわりもぞする

ONE   HUNDRED   POEMS
FROM
ONE   HUNDRED   POETS

How wet my sleeves with dew of night,

For in this ill-thatched cot I sleep,

Guarding the fields of autumn bright

With grain for farmers now to reap.

秋の田の
かりほの庵の
苫をあらみ
わが衣手は
つゆにぬれつゝ

天智天皇

Aki no ta no kari ho no iho no toma wo arami

Waga koromode wa tsuyu ni nure tsutsu

—*The Emperor Tenchi*

Spring is already gone and now

    It seems the summer's come, for lo,

All white is yonder Kagu's brow

    With garments airing row on row.

持統天皇

春すぎて
夏きにけらし
白妙の

衣ほすてふ
あまの香具山

Haru sugite natsu ki ni kerashi shirotae no
    Koromo hosu chyô ama-no-kagu yama

—*The Empress Jito*

Oh, no one knows how me it ails

　　To lie in bed and thus to brood

All night which seems long as the tails

　　Of mountain pheasants of the wood.

柿本人麿

あし曳の
山鳥の尾の
しだり尾の
ながながし夜を
ひとりかもねん

Ashibiki no yamadori no o no shidari o no

Naganaga shi yo wo hitori kamo nen

—*Kakinomoto-no Hitomaro*

From Tago Beach I view the sight,

Above the clouds, of Fuji's brow

Sublime, all covered with the white

Of snow that seems there falling now.

山邊赤人

田子の浦に
打ち出でゝ見れば
白妙の

ふじのたかねに
雪はふりつゝ

Tago no ura ni uchi idede mireba shirotae no
Fuji no takane ni yuki wa furi tsutsu

—*Yamabe-no Akahito*

When in the forest deep and red

    I hear the plaintive cries of deer,

As, wandering, on the leaves they tread,

    Then autumn seems indeed so drear.

猿丸太夫

おくやまに
紅葉ふみわけ
なく鹿の
こゑきく時ぞ
秋はかなしき

Oku yama ni momiji fumi wake naku shika no

    Koe kiku toki zo aki wa kanashiki

—Sarumaru

I look up at the starry sky,

And see the frost laid clear and white

Upon the Magpie Bridge on high

To know how far spent is the night.

中納言家持

かさゝぎの
渡せる橋に
おくしもの

白きを見れば
夜ぞふけにける

Kasasagi no wataseru hashi ni oku shimo no

Shiroki wo mireba yo zo fuke ni keru

—*Ohtomo-no Yakamochi*

Behold, the moon now rises clear—

The selfsame moon the people find

At Kasuga town, my home, appear

From old Mt. Mikasa behind.

安倍仲麿

天の原
ふりさけみれば
春日なる
三笠の山に
出でし月かも

Ama no hara furisake mireba kasuga naru

Mikasa no yama ni ideshi tsuki kamo

—*Abe-no Nakamaro*

Here on a mountain do I stay,

South-east of the capital,

In hermitage forlorn and grey—

Upon Mt. Drear, so called by all.

喜撰法師

わがいほは
都のたつみ
しかぞすむ

世を宇治山と
人は云ふなり

Waga iho wa miyako no tatsumi shika zo sumu

Yo wo Uji yama to hito wa iu nari

—*The Priest Kisen*

As in the long and weary rain

The hue of flowers is all gone,

So is my young grace spent in vain

In these long years I lived alone.

花の色は
移りにけりな
いたづらに
わが身世にふる
眺めせしまに

小野小町

Hana no iro wa utsuri ni keri na itazura ni
Waga mi yo ni furu nagame sehi ma ni

—*Ono-no Komachi*

Lo, at this barrier people greet,

Those leaving home, and those who hope

Home to return; so it is meet

To call the barrier Trysting Slope.

蟬丸

これやこの
行くも歸るも
別れては
知るも知らぬも
あふさかの關

Kore ya kono yuku mo kaeru mo wakarete wa
Shiru mo shiranu mo ôsaka no seki

—*Semimaru*

O Fisherman, tell it for me

To my dear folks at home that I

Set out alone across the sea

For Isles which far off groupèd lie.

和田の原
八十島かけて
こぎ出ぬと
人には告げよ
あまのつりぶね

参議篁

Wada no hara yasoshima kakete kogi idenu to

Hito ni wa tsugeyo ama no tsuribune

—*Ono-no Takamura*

O Heaven's Wind, be kind and close

    The gate whereby clouds pass away,

For lo, the maiden dancing goes,—

    The maiden beautiful and gay.

僧正遍照

あまつ風
雲の通ひ路
ふきとぢよ
乙女の姿
しばしとゞめん

Amatsu kaze kumo no kayoiji fuki tojiyo

Otome no sugata shibashi todomen

—*The Priest Henjo*

As fast the Mina Stream is brought

Down, down Mt. Tsukuba to fall

Into deep pools there to be caught,

So love profound holds me in thrall.

筑波嶺の
みねより落つる
みなの川
こひぞつもりて
淵となりぬる

陽成院

Tsukuba ne no mine yori otsuru mina no gawa

Koi zo tsumorite fuchi to nari nuru

—*The Retired Emperor Yôzei*

Oh, why am I in such a plight?

    Like the cloth patterns all confused

Of Shinobu with colours bright,

    For you, alas, I'm so bemused.

河原左大臣

みちのくの
しのぶもぢずり
たれ故に
亂れそめにし
われならなくに

Michinoku no shinobu moji-zuri tare yue ni
Midare some nishi ware naranaku ni

—Minamoto-no **Toru**

Out in the field of spring I go

　　To gather young herbs for your sake,

But now, alas, here comes the snow

　　To wet my coat-sleeves with its flake.

君がため
春の野に出でゝ
若菜つむ

わが衣手に
雪はふりつゝ

光孝天皇

Kimi ga tame haru no no ni idete wakana tsumu

Waga koromode ni yuki wa furi tsutsu

　　　　　　　—The Emperor Koko

Now I shall leave, but do not grieve.

If like the wellknown mountain tree

You *pine* indeed for me, I'll speed

Homeward wherever I may be.

中納言行平

たち別れ
いなばの山の
峯におふる

まつとしきかば
今かへりこん

Tachi wakare inaba no yama no mine ni ôru

Matsu to shi kikaba ima kaeri kon

—*Ariwara-no Yukihira*

How fair the Tatsuta, for lo,

    Was the stream ever carpeted,

Even when Gods were here below,

    With such bright maple-leaves and red?

在原業平

ちはやふる
神代もきかず
龍田川
からくれないに
水くゝるとは

Chihaya furu kami yo mo kikazu tatsuta gawa

Kara kurenai ni mizu kuguru to wa

—*Ariwara-no Narihira*

(17)

By day, alas, well do I know

I must shun people and their eye

When to meet my love I go;

But must I be in dreams so shy?

すみの江の
岸による浪
よるさへや
ゆめのかよひ路
人めよくらん

敏行朝臣

Sumi-no-ye no kishi ni yoru nami yoru sae ya

Yume no kayoi-ji hito-me yokuran

—*Fujiwara-no Toshiyuki*

Oh, come to me, for I must needs

    Behold you.　Even for a space

As that between the joints of reeds

    Fail not to come to me apace.

伊勢

なには潟
みじかきあしの
ふしのまも
逢はでこのよを
過してよとや

Naniwa gata mijikaki ashi no fushi no ma mo

Awade kono yo wo sugoshite yo to ya

—*Princess Ise*

Weary my mind and all cast down;

And like the watermarks we see

At Naniwa if I must drown

To meet her, I will die in glee.

元良親王

わびぬれば
今はたおなじ
難波なる
みをつくしても
逢はんとぞ思ふ

Wabi nureba ima hata onaji naniwa naru

Mi wo tsukushite mo awan to zo omou

—*The Heir-Apparent Motoyoshi*

She promised me to come here soon,

And eager I await her call,

Yet who comes but the morning moon?

And oh, no sight of her at all.

素性法師

今こんと
いひしばかりに
なが月の
有明の月を
待ちいづるかな

Ima kon to iishi bakari ni naga-tsuki no

Ariake no tsuki wo machi izuru kana

—*The Priest Sosei*

Tree leaves and grass from withering die

When mountain winds come in the fall.

And well the wind may be called high

That comes down blowing over all.

吹
く
か
ら
に
秋
の
草
木
の
し
を
る
れ
ば

む
べ
山
風
を
嵐
と
い
ふ
ら
ん

文
屋
康
秀

Fuku kara ni aki no kusa ki no shiorureba

Mube yama kaze wo arashi to iuran

—*Bunya-no Yasuhide*

Whene'er the autumn moon I see

Pathos soon comes me to enthrall,

Though I'm aware not only me

But to us all does come the fall.

わが身ひとつの
秋にはあらねど

ちゞにものこそ
悲しけれ

月みれば

大江千里

Tsuki mireba chiji ni mono koso kanashi kere

Waga mi hitotsu no aki ni wa aranedo

—*Oe-no Chisato*

I bring no offerings to thy shrine,

    For with the Sovereign now I be;

But here the maple leaves so fine

    Better than aught will pleasure thee.

菅家

このたびは
幣もとりあへず
手向山
もみぢのにしき
神のまにまに

Kono tabi wa nusa mo tori-aezu tamuke-yama

Momiji no nishiki kami no mani mani

—*Sugawara-no Michizane*

If you knew how much I love you,

    You would not fail to come to me.

Will no prayer of mine e'er move you

    To come and see me secretly?

三條右大臣

名にしおはゞ
逢坂山の
さねかづら
人にしられで
くるよしもがな

Na ni shi owaba ôsaka yama no sanekazura

    Hito ni shirarede kuru yoshi mo gana

—*The Minister Sadakata*

If for us, Maple leaves, you care,

That now Mt. Ogura adorn,

Wait for our Sovereign's visit ere

You fall, and leave the peak forlorn.

小倉山　　貞信公

峯のもみぢば

心あらば

いまひとたびの

みゆきまたなん

Ogura yama mine no momiji-ba kokoro araba

Ima hito tabi no miyuki matanan

—*Prince Teishin*

When, I wonder, did I greet her?

　　All's gone out of my memory.

Still I long and yearn to meet her

　　Beside the stream of Izumi.

中納言兼輔

みかの原
湧きて流るゝ
いづみ川

いつみきとてか
戀しかるらん

Mika no hara wakite nagaruru Izumi gawa

　Itsu mikitote ka koishi karuran

—*Kanesuke*

Of all the seasons of the year

    Winter in mountain hamlets bare

Is the most forlorn and drear,

    Since men and grass then are so rare.

源宗干朝臣

やま里は
冬ぞさびしさ
まさりける

人めも草も
枯れぬとおもへば

Yama zato wa fuyu zo sabishisa masari keru

    Hito-me mo kusa mo karenu to omoeba

               —*Minamoto-no Muneyuki*

The year's first frost this morning fell,

    And I who seek some flowers white

Of my chrysanthemums can't tell

    The blossom from the rime aright.

凡河內躬恒

こゝろあてに
折らばや折らむ
初霜の

置きまどはせる
しら菊の花

Kokoro ate ni orabaya oran hatsu shimo no

    Oki madowaseru shira giku no hana

                —*Oshikochi-no Mitsune*

Since I experienced to my grief

That parting in the early morn,

Naught is so sad in my belief

As morning moon, and so forlorn.

有明の
つれなくみえし
わかれより
あかつきばかり
憂きものはなし

壬生忠岑

Ariake no tsurenaku mieshi wakare yori

Akatsuki bakari uki mono wa nashi

—*Mibu-no Tadamine*

The moon at Yoshino, how bright!

I marvelled at the break of day,

And looked to see the town so light

In falling snow's serene array.

坂上是則

あさぼらけ
有明の月と
みるまでに

吉野の里に
降れるしらゆき

Asaborake ariake no tsuki to miru made ni

Yoshino no sato ni fureru shira yuki

—*Sakanouye-no Korenori*

Who laid this hurdle fair and red

Here in the mountain rivulet?

'Tis but the mischievous wind that led

The fallen leaves in drifts to set.

山かはに
風のかけたる
しがらみは
流れもあへぬ
もみぢなりけり

春道列樹

Yama kawa ni kaze no kaketaru shigarami wa

Nagare mo aenu momiji nari keri

—*Harumichi-no Tsuraki*

Upon this sunlit vernal day

    The cherry flowers give me pain.

Why on their boughs can they not stay?

    Why shower the petals down like rain?

ひさかたの
光のどけき
春の日に
しづ心なく
花の散るらん

紀友則

Hisakata no hikari nodokeki haru no hi ni
Shizu kokoro naku hana no chiruran

—*Ki-no Tomonori*

I mourn a host of old friends gone;

    Alas, I have outlived them all.

The old pines on the hill alone

    Stand there forlorn, deaf to my call.

誰
れ
を
か
も
知
る
人
に
せ
む
高
砂
の

ま
つ
も
む
か
し
の
友
な
ら
な
く
に

藤
原
興
風

Tare wo kamo shiru hito ni sen takasago no

    Matsu mo mukashi no tomo nara naku ni

                  —*Fujiwara-no Okikaze*

How the village friend may meet me

I know not, but the old plum flowers

Still now with their fragrance greet me

Kindly as in the bygone hours.

花ぞ昔の
香ににほひける

心も知らず
ふるさとは

ひとはいさ

紀貫之

Hito wa isa kokoro mo shirazu furu sato wa

Hana zo mukashi no ka ni nioi keru

—*Ki-no Tsurayuki*

The day soon breaks in summertide

    Even while night seems young as yet;

And does the moon forlornly ride

    Cloud-hidden till it comes to set?

清原深養父

夏の夜は
まだ宵ながら
明けぬるを
くものいづこに
月やどるらん

Natsu no yo wa mada yoi nagara akenuru wo

Kumo no izuko ni tsuki yadoruran

              —*Kiyowara-no Fukayabu*

Cold the autumn wind is blowing,

Scattering the dew about the lea.

And here I see the gusts now sowing

Rare unstringèd pearls free.

文屋朝康

しらつゆに
風のふきしく
秋の野は

つらぬきとめぬ
玉ぞちりける

Shira tsuyu ni kaze no fukishiku aki no no wa

Tsuranuki tomenu tama zo chiri keru

—*Bunya-no Asayasu*

Let him forget me, if he please,

But to the gods he made a vow;

And how their anger to appease

Is what I'm worrying for him now.

右近

わすらるゝ
身をば思はず
誓ひてし

人のいのちの
惜しくもあるかな

Wasuraruru mi wo ba omowazu chikaite shi

Hito no inochi no oshiku mo aru kana

—*The Lady Ukon*

I try my feelings to conceal,

    But deep, sweet, is my love for you

And 'twill in vain itself reveal,

    Leaving me but to sigh in rue.

参議等

浅茅生の
小野のしの原
しのぶれど

あまりてなどか
人のこひしき

Asajifu no ono no shinowara shinoburedo

Amarite nado ka hito no koishiki

—*Minamoto-no Hitoshi*

Hard though I try my love to hide,

The telltale blushes soon betray;

And people ask what I abide

That causes me to waste away.

忍ふれど
色に出にけり
わが戀は
ものやおもふと
人のとふまで

平兼盛

Shinoburedo iro ni de ni keri waga koi wa

Mono ya omou to hito no tou made

—*Taira-no Kanemori*

Ill news indeed will run apace;

For though I loved so secretly,

Word is abroad of my disgrace.

And oh, forlorn now I must cry.

人知れずこそ
思ひそめしが

我が名はまだき
たちにけり

戀すてふ

壬生忠見

Koi su chô waga na wa madaki tachi ni keri

Hito shirezu koso omoi someshi ga

—*Mibu-no Tadami*

Soaking with flowing tears our sleeve,

We vowed that we should love on still,

Though waves rise and no traces leave

Of our love-trysting pine-clad hill.

契りきな
かたみに袖を
しぼりつゝ
すゑの松山
浪こさじとは

清原元輔

Chigiriki na katami ni sode wo shibori tsutsu

Sue no matsu yama nami kosaji to wa

—*Kiyowara-no Motosuke*

How happy was I in those days

    Ere of her yet I had no sight!

I live in sorrow now that preys

    Upon my heart by day and night.

中納言敦忠

あひみての
後の心に
くらぶれば

むかし
はものを
思はざりけり

Ai mite no nochi no kokoro ni kurabureba

    Mukashi wa mono wo omowazari keri

—*Atsutada*

If man and woman did not meet,

Never sorrow would them bother;

The love-tryst, then, can not be sweet,

When it grieves one and the other.

中納言朝忠

あふことの
絶えて
しなくば

なかなかに

人をもみをも

うらみざらまし

Au koto no taete shi nakuba naka naka ni

Hito wo mo mi wo mo uramizarama shi

—*Chunagon Asatada*

(44)

Worthy of her I try to prove,

But she is cold to me, and scorned

Thus in my unrequited love

Oh, I shall pass away unmourned.

謙徳公

あはれとも
いふべき人は
おもほえて
みのいたづらに
なりぬべきかな

Aware to mo iu beki hito wa omohoete

Mi no itazura ni narinu beki kana

—*Prince Kentoku*

The wretched boatmen do not know,

　　Their rudder gone at Yura Strait,

Where will their drifting vessel go.

　　And where my love, and to what fate?

曾根好忠

由良の戸を
渡る舟人
梶をたえ

ゆくえも知らぬ
こひの道かな

Yura no to wo wataru funabito kaji wo tae

Yukue mo shiranu koi no michi kana

—*Sone Yoshitada*

Wretched is my cottage where

　　Only the cleavers hold their sway.

And to this bower lorn and bare

　　In secret comes the autumn grey.

八重むぐら
しげれる宿の
　　寂しさに
ひとこそみえね
秋はきにけり

惠慶法師

Yaemugura shigereru yado no sabishisa ni

Hito koso miene aki wa ki ni keri

—*The Priest Ekei*

As the wind-driven billows shriek

    Against the rocks and vainly break,

So, though to win you hard I seek,

    You'll not be shaken for my sake.

風をいたみ
岩うつなみの
おのれのみ
くだけて物を
おもふころかな

源重之

Kaze wo itami iwa utsu nami no onore nomi

    Kudakete mono wo omou koro kana

—*Minamoto-no Shigeyuki*

Like watch fires burning bright to light

    The men who guard the palace ground,

My bosom glows aflame by night,

    And wastes by day in grief profound.

物をこそおもへ　ひるは消えつゝ　よは燃えて　衛士の焚く火の　御垣守　大中臣能宣

Mikaki mori eji no taku hi no yo wa moete

  Hiru wa kie tsutsu mono wo koso omoe

        —*Yoshinobu*

Before I came to know you, love,

Little my life was worth to me.

I prize it now all things above,

And wish long in this world to be.

君がため
惜しからざりし
命さへ

ながくもがなと
思ひけるかな

藤原義孝

Kimi ga tame oshikarazarishi inochi sae

Nagaku mogana to omoi keru kana

—*Fujiwara-no Yoshitaka*

Oh, does she know I suffer so

From fire which in my heart doth burn,

Blazing ever, ceasing never,

Only because for her I yearn?

かくとだに
えやはいぶきの
さしも草
さしもしらじな
もゆるおもひを

藤原實方朝臣

Kaku to dani eyawa Ibuki no sashi-mogusa

Sashimo shiraji na moyuru omoi wo

—*Fujiwara-no Sanekata*

If day breaks, I am well aware

　　Night soon will come to us again,

And yet I find it hard to bear

　　Our parting and lament in vain.

明けぬれば
くるゝものとは
知りながら
なほうらめしき
朝ぼらけかな

藤原道信朝臣

Akenureba kururu mono to wa shiri nagara

　　Nao urameshiki asaborake kana

—*Fujiwara-no Michinobu*

The night seems long, you are aware,

　　When in your bed you lie awake,

Sighing, weeping, full of care,

　　Waiting for the day to break.

歎きつゝ
ひとりぬる夜の
　明くるまは
いかに久しき
ものとかはしる

右大將道綱母

Nageki tsutsu hitori nuru yo no akuru ma wa

　Ikani hisashiki mono to kawa shiru

—*The Mother of Michitsuna*

Not that your words I disbelieve,

But that the minds of men do change.

Therefore I wish to die this eve

Ere you from me yourself estrange.

わすれじの行末までは かたければ 今日を限りの 命ともがな

儀同三司母

Wasureji no yukusue made wa katakereba

Kyo wo kagiri no inochi tomo gana

—*The Mother of Korechika*

Although for long the booming sound

Of our old Fall has been unheard,

I know that in the stream is found

Its great renown as yet unblurred.

大納言公任

たきの音は
絶えて久しく
成りぬれど
名こそ流れて
なほきこえけれ

Taki no oto wa taete hisashiku narinuredo

Na koso nagarete nao kikoe kere

—*Dainagon Kinto*

My sands of life are running low,

　　So grant me now my one request,

And let me see you ere I go

　　Well to remember when I rest.

和泉式部

あらざらん この世の外の　思ひ出に　今ひとたびの　逢ふこともがな

Arazaran kono yo no hoka no omoide ni
Ima hito tabi no au koto mo gana

—*The Lady Izumi Shikibu*

After long years we met, O Moon,

And how I wished to have him stay;

But as you hide in clouds too soon,

So did he likewise go away.

雲かくれにし
夜半の月かな

見しやそれとも
わかぬまに

めぐり逢ひて

紫式部

Meguri aite mishi ya sore tomo wakanu ma ni
Kumo kakure nishi yowa no tsuki kana

—*The Lady Murasaki Shikibu*

Shall I forget you, love? oh, nay!

Nor shall I e'er my pledge forsake.

But if you should my love betray—

'Tis this that makes my poor heart ache!

いでそよ人を
忘れやはする

ゐなのさゝ原
風ふけば

ありま山

大貳三位

Arima yama ina no sasawara kaze fukeba

Ide soyo hito wo wasure yawa suru

—*The Lady Katako, Daini Sammi*

Alas, if only I had known

That you could be so false to me,

I'd not have sat up all alone

In vain the setting moon to see.

赤染衛門

やすらはで
ねなましものを
さ夜ふけて
かたぶくまでの
月をみしかな

Yasurawade nenamashi mono wo sayo fukete

Katabuku made no tsuki wo mishi kana

—The Lady Akazome Emon

My mother's gone away, alas,

And now great distance lies between,

And many days and months must pass

Before her words come to be seen.

小式部内侍

大江山
いく野の道の
とほければ
まだふみもみず
天の橋立

Ohye yama ikuno no michi no toh kereba

Mada fumi mo mizu ama-no-hashidate

—*Lady-in-Waiting Koshikibu*

The double cherry blossoms, lo,

    Of Nara, the ancient capital,

Now in the Imperial Palace blow,

    Glorious and sweet before us all.

けふ九重に
にほひぬるかな

いにしへの
奈良の都の
八重櫻

伊勢大輔

Inishie no nara no miyako no yae-zakura

    Kyô kokonoe ni nioi nuru kana

            —*The Lady Ise-no Ohsuke*

The cock's cry one might imitate

Barriers to pass before sunrise,

But oh, to cross my barrier-gate

What power of yours can well devise?

夜をこめて
鳥のそらねは
はかるとも
よにあふさかの
關はゆるさじ

清少納言

Yo wo komete tori no sorane wa hakaru tomo

Yo ni Osaka no seki wa yurusaji

—*The Lady Sei Shonagon*

Alas, I have to give her up,

Try to endure whatever pain;

But ere I drink this fateful cup,

Oh, let me see her once again.

いまはたゞ
思ひ絶えなんと
　　ばかりを
人づてならで
いふよしもがな

左京大夫道雅

Ima wa tada omoi taenan to bakari wo

Hito zute narade iu yoshi mo gana

—*Sakyo Dayu Michimasa*

Now in the Uji River where

The rolling mist has gone from view

Appears clear in the morning air

The basket-work of split bamboo.

あ
ら
は
れ
渡
る

瀬
々
の
あ
じ
ろ
ぎ

あ
さ
ぼ
ら
け

宇
治
の
川
霧

た
え
だ
え
に

權
中
納
言
定
頼

Asaborake uji no kawagiri tae dae ni

Araware wataru zeze no ajiro-gi

—Gon Chunagon Sadayori

Ah, my heart, my heart is broken,

Sodden are my sleeves with brine;

Ne'er I hear my name now spoken

Save as a secret gibe malign.

恨みわび
ほさぬ袖だに
あるものを
こひに朽ちなん
名こそおしけれ

相模

Urami wabi hosanu sode dani aru mono wo

Koi ni kuchinan na koso oshikere

—*The Lady Sagami*

I pray, O fair wild Cherry Tree

That stand alone upon the peak,

Let us be of one mind, for we

Are friendless both, forlorn and weak.

花 諸 前
よ 共 大
り あ に 僧
ほ は 正
知 か れ 行
る に と 尊
人 山 お
も ざ も
な く へ
し ら

Morotomo ni aware to omoe yama zakura

Hana yori hoka ni shiru hito mo nashi

—The Former Archibishop Gyoson

I laid my head upon an arm

A little while one night of spring,

And now, alas, must feel alarm

At the dread rumour on the wing.

春の夜の
夢ばかりなる
手まくらに
かひなくたゝむ
名こそをしけれ

周防內侍

Haru no yo no yume bakari naru ta-makura ni

Kainaku tatan na koso oshi kere

—*The Lady-in-Waiting Suwo*

Harassed with much chagrin and care,

I live on still, yet in my sight

The moon this midnight looks so fair

There in the heavens shining bright.

心にも
あらで浮き世に
ながらへば

こひしかるべき
夜半の月かな

三條院

Kokoro ni mo arade uki yo ni nagaraeba
Koishikarubeki yowa no tsuki kana

—The Emperor Sanjo

Across Mt. Mimuro did blow

The wind, scattering leaves so red,

And on the stream of Tatta, lo,

A fine brocade is overspread.

あらしふく
三室の山の
もみぢば は

籠田の川の
にしきなりけり

能因法師

Arashi fuku mimuro no yama no momiji-ba wa

Tatsuta no kawa no nishiki nari keri

—*The Priest Nôin*

Sad, I wandered out, and weary,

To soothe my mind, but everywhere

Did I see the shadows dreary

Of autumn twilight in the air.

良暹法師

寂しさに
宿をたち出でゝ
ながむれば
いづこもおなじ
秋の夕ぐれ

Sabishisa ni yado wo tachi-idete nagamureba

Izuko mo onaji aki no yugure

—*The Priest Ryôsen*

Courteous the autumn breeze and sweet;

On making farms a twilight call,

First farmers' rice-ears it will greet,

Then go into their reed-thatched hall.

大納言經信

ゆふされば
門田の稲葉
おとづれて

あし
のまろ屋に
秋風ぞふく

Yusareba kado-da no inaba otozurete

Ashi no maroya ni aki kaze zo fuku

—*Minamoto-no Tsunenobu*

Do you ever wish to love me?

You are aware 'tis I who grieve.

Never, therefore, seek to move me,

And, pray, unsodden leave my sleeve!

かけじや袖の
ぬれもこそすれ

たかしの濱の
あだ波は

おとにきく

祐子内親王紀伊

Oto ni kiku takashi no hama no adanami wa

Kakeji ya sode no nure mo koso sure

—*The Lady Kii*

I see the cherry-trees so fair

On yonder hillsides all abloom.

Let not the fog now come and dare

To veil the nearer hills in gloom.

高砂の
尾の上のさくら
咲きにけり

外山のかすみ
たゝずもあらなむ

前中納言匡房

Takasago no onoe no sakura saki ni keri

Toyama no kasumi tatazu mo aranan

—*Ohye-no Masafusa*

Blow, gently, Wind, down Hasse's peak

Where the old temple we behold.

I came to pray my love be meek,

And not so hard as you and cold.

源俊頼朝臣

うかりける
人を初瀬の
山おろし

はげしかれとは
祈らぬものを

Ukari keru hito wo hasse no yama oroshi

Hageshi kare to wa inoranu mono wo

—*Minamoto-no Toshiyori*

Upon your word do I rely,

As grass on dew from day to day,

But you have made me no reply,

And autumn soon will pass away.

藤原基俊

ちぎり置きし
させもが露を
命にて

あはれことしの
秋もいぬめり

Chigiri okishi sasemo ga tsuyu wo inochi nite

Aware kotoshi no aki mo inumeri

—*Fujiwara-no Mototoshi*

I have rowed out, and yonder where

    The boundless ocean meets the sky

I see the billows white and fair

    Leaping against the clouds on high.

法性寺入道
前關白太政大臣

わだの原

漕ぎ出でゝみれば

久方の

雲井にまがふ

沖津白なみ

Wada no hara kogi idete mireba hisakata no

    Kumoi ni magoh okitsu shira nami

—*Tadamichi*

As water of a stream will meet,

Though, barred by rocks, apart it fall

In rash cascades, so we too, sweet,

Shall be together after all.

崇徳院

瀬を早み
岩にせかるゝ
たき川の
われても末に
あはんとぞ思ふ

Sewo hayami iwa ni sekaruru taki-gawa no

Warete mo sue ni awan to zo omou

—*The Retired Emperor Sutoku*

Across the stilly air of night

    Awaji-wards the plovers fly,

And barrier-keepers sleeping light

    Are oft awakened by their cry.

源
兼
昌

あ
は
ぢ
島
通
ふ
千
鳥
の
　
な
く
聲
に

い
く
夜
ね
ざ
め
ぬ
須
磨
の
關
守

Awaji shima kayou chidori no naku koe ni

  Iku yo nezamenu suma no seki-mori

          —Minamoto-no Kanemasa

Out of the rifts of clouds of night

    There by the wind of autumn blown

Appears the moon so fair and bright,

    Sailing the misty skies alone.

左京大夫顕輔

あき風に
たなびく雲の
たえ間より

もれ出る月の
影のさやけさ

Aki kaze ni tanabiku kumo no taema yori

More-izuru tsuki no kage no sayakesa

—*Akisuke*

If he be true I'm unaware;

But since the dawn saw him depart,

As all dishevelled is my hair,

So in confusion is my heart.

待賢門院堀川

ながからむ
こゝろもしらず
黒髪の

みだれてけさは
物をこそおもへ

Nagakaran kokoro mo shirazu kuro kami no

Midarete kesa wa mono wo koso omoe

— *Lady Horikawa*

I hear a cuckoo in the sky,

But when I seek to spot the call,

Only the morning moon's on high,

And of the bird no sign at all.

後徳大寺左大臣

ほととぎす
なきつる方を
眺むれば
たゞ有明の
月ぞのこれる

Hototogisu nakitsuru kata wo nagamureba

Tada ariake no tsuki zo nokoreru

—*Gotokudaiji Sanesada*

I live on, thinking life is vain,

And tired of lover's care, but still

'Tis strange that I can not refrain

From tears, which come against my will.

おもひわび　さても命は　あるものを　うきに堪へぬは　なみだなりけり

道因法師

Omoi wabi satemo inochi wa aru mono wo

Uki ni taenu wa namida nari keri

—*The Priest Dôin*

How can I from my sorrow flee?

For though I'm in the mountains drear,

There's no surcease of grief for me,

And still the deer's sad cries I hear.

皇太后宮大夫俊成

世の中よ
道こそなけれ
思ひいる

やまの奥にも
鹿ぞなくなる

Yo no naka yo michi koso nakere omoi iru

Yama no oku ni mo shika zo naku naru

—*Fujiwara-no Toshinari*

If only these days I survive,

I shall enjoy their memory;

For with regret I keep alive

The weary bygone days in me.

うしと見し世ぞ
今はこひしき
しと見し世ぞ

しのばれん
まだこの頃や
ながらへば

藤原清輔朝臣

Nagaraeba mada konogoro ya shinobaren

Ushi to mishi yozo ima wa koishiki

—*Fujiwara-no Kiyosuke*

It seems the day will never break,

As sad I lie the livelong night.

Even the door-chinks make me ache,

Because they will let in no light.

よもすがら
物思ふ頃は
明けやらで
閨のひまさへ
つれなかりけり

俊惠法師

Yomosugara mono omou koro wa ake yarade

Neya no hima sae tsurena kari keri

—*The Priest Shunye*

Oh, never call the moon perverse,

Because she makes us feel so drear.

We weep unbidden, and lay the curse

Upon her for our eyes turned blear.

なげけとて
月やは物を
思はする
かこち顔なる
わが涙かな

西行法師

Nageke tote tsuki ya wa mono wo omowasuru

Kakochi-gao naru waga namida kana

—*The Priest Saigyo*

How fair the twilight of the fall!

    After the shower a vapour fine

Arises from the earth to crawl

    And veil the sodden leaves of pine.

むら雨の
露もまだひぬ
まきの葉に
きり立ちのぼる
秋の夕ぐれ

寂蓮法師

Murasame no tsuyu mo mada hinu maki no ha ni
    Kiri tachi noboru aki no yugure

—*The Priest Jyakuren*

By Naniwa Canal where thrive

　　The reeds I spent a happy night,

And ever while I am alive

　　I shall keep hoping for his sight.

難波江の
あしのかりねの
　ひとよゆゑ
みをつくしてや
戀ひわたるべき

皇嘉門院別當

Naniwa e no ashi no karine no hito yo yue
Mi wo tsukushite ya koi wataru beki

—Daughter of Toshitaka

Oh, let me die! What do I care?

For if I live, I only strive

In vain and peak in love, aware

My heart's dead, though I be alive.

式子内親王

玉の緒よ
絶えなば絶えね
長らへば
しのぶることの
よわりもぞする

Tama no o yo taenaba taene nagaraeba

Shinoburu koto no yowari mo zo suru

—*Princess Shikishi*

Though wet with spray, the divers' sleeve

Will never change its hue as mine;

For lo, I yearn for you and grieve

To see my robes all soiled with brine.

見せばやな
雄島のあまの
袖だにも
ぬれにぞぬれし
色はかはらじ

殷富門院大輔

Misebayana ojima no ama no sode dani mo

Nure ni zo nureshi iro wa kawaraji

—*Princess Sukeko*

Alas, upon this frosty eve

   The crickets chirp so wearily;

And cold I lie upon my sleeve,

   Hearing the insect's plaintive cry.

後京極攝政太政大臣

きりぎりす
なくや霜夜の
さむしろに

衣片しき
ひとりかもねん

Kirigirisu naku ya shimo yo no samushiro ni

Koromo katashiki hitori kamo nen

—Gokyogoku Yoshitsune

My sleeves are like the rocks that lie

Hidden even at low tide,

And have no moment to be dry:

Unknown this doom must they abide!

二條院讃岐

わが袖は
汐干に見えぬ
おきの石の
人こそ知らね
かわくまもなし

Waga sode wa shiohi ni mienu oki no ishi no

Hito koso shirane kawaku ma mo nashi

—*The Lady Sanuki*

O for longevity! No speech

    Can tell this love for life of mine;

Even yon boat along the beach

    The men are dragging looks so fine.

鎌倉右大臣

世の中は
常にもがもな
なぎさこぐ
あまのをぶねの
綱手かなしも

Yo no naka wa tsune ni mo gamo na nagisa kogu

    Ama no obune no tsunade kanashi mo

—*Minamoto-no Sanetomo*

How cold the autumn wind and drear

    Now blowing down Mt. Yoshino,

And somewhere in the town I hear

    The sound of beating linen go.

参議雅經

みよし野の
山のあき風
さよふけて
ふるさと寒く
衣うつなり

Miyoshino no yama no aki kaze sayo fukete
Furu sato samuku koromo utsu nari

—*Masatsune*

Oh, how profound is my delight

That for all fellow-creatures now

I, though a poor priest, can recite

The prayers upon this mountain brow!

前大僧正慈圓

おふけなく
うき世の民に
おほふかな

わが立つそまに
すみぞめの袖

Ohkenaku uki yono tami ni oho kana

Waga tatsu soma ni sumizome no sode

—The Former Archibishop Jien

(95)

'Tis not the snow by tempests blown

Of cherries falling to the ground,

But me I grieve so aged grown

Soon to be in a sleep profound.

入道前太政大臣

花さそふ
あらしの庭の
雪ならで
ふりゆくものは
わが身なりけり

Hana sasou arashi no niwa no yuki narade

Furi yuku mono wa waga mi nari keri

—*Saionji Kintsune*

Weary it is indeed to yearn

For one who comes not for my sake:

My heart's afire like weeds they burn

That salt they in that wise may take.

權中納言定家

こぬ人を
まつほのうらの
夕なぎに

燒くやも鹽の
身もこがれつゝ

Konu hito wo matsu-ho no ura no yunagi ni

Yaku ya mo shio no mi mo kogare tsutsu

—*Fujiwara-no Sadaiye*

Though cool the breeze athwart the trees,

I see some bathers in the stream.

But for their sight in this twilight,

Spring is the season it would seem.

従二位家隆

風そよぐ
奈良の小川の
夕ぐれは

みそぎぞ夏の
しるしなりけり

Kaze soyogu nara no ogawa no yugure wa
Misogi zo natsu no shirushi nari keri

—*Iyetaka*

How I adore the men of yore,

    And pity those who live today;

I muse in pain on life in vain,

    And have, alas, of hope no ray.

後鳥羽院　　ひともをし　　　あぢきなく　　世をおもふ故に　　もの思ふ身は
　　　　　　人も恨めし

Hito mo oshi hito mo urameshi ajiki naku

    Yo wo omou yue ni mono omou mi wa

    —*The Retired Emperor Gotoba*

Never the palace I behold

But pathos seizes soon on me;

And I regret the days of old

Upon its eaves the ferns to see.

順德院

ももしきや

ふるき軒端の

しのぶにも

なほあまりある

昔なりけり

Momoshiki ya furuki nokiba no shinobu ni mo

Nao amari aru mukashi nari keri

—*The Retired Emperor Juntoku*

APPENDIX

THE RHYME SCHEME

An English friend of mine once wondered if these songs could not be rendered in such a way as to enable English readers to play cards with them just as we do in Japanese. And this I hope I have attained to some extent in the present attempt. The rhyme scheme of each quatrain is a, b, a, b: the first line of the upper part or *kami-no-ku* rhymes with that of the lower part or *shimo-no-ku,* and the second line with the last. There are, however, a few exceptions in which internal rhymes in the first and third lines take the place of end-rhymes. These are puzzle cards, if they may be so called, and will make the game more amusing, if confusing.

HOW TO PLAY POETRY CARDS

Two sets of cards, the reading cards and the playing cards, consisting of one hundred cards respectively, are used. On the reading card the whole poem is written or printed, while on the playing card only the last two lines are given.

The game is usually played between two parties

made up of four or five persons. Each party faces the other with fifty playing cards spread before them on the floor. As the reader recites one of the well-shuffled reading cards, the players try to find and take the corresponding playing card faster than the others. In this way the party that has first finished with their allotted cards wins.

ONE HUNDRED POEMS FROM
ONE HUNDRED POETS
小倉百人一首

1956年12月28日　初版発行　　　　1991年7月25日　18刷発行

検印省略

著　者　本　多　平　八　郎
発行者　株式会社 北星堂書店
代表者　山　本　雅　三
〒113 東京都文京区本郷駒込3-32-4
Tel(03)3827-0511　Fax(03)3827-0567

THE HOKUSEIDO PRESS
32-4, Honkomagome 3-chome, Bunkyo-ku, Tokyo　113 Japan

❖落丁・乱丁本はお取替いたします。